Decomposers

Megan Lappi

WEIGL PUBLISHERS INC.

Published by Weigl Publishers Inc.
350 5th Avenue, Suite 3304, PMB 6G
New York, NY 10118-0069 USA
Web site: www.weigl.com

Library of Congress Cataloging-in-Publication Data

Lappi, Megan.
  Decomposers / Megan Lappi.
     p. cm. -- (Nature's food chain)
  Includes index.
  ISBN 1-59036-239-X (lib. bdg. : alk. paper) 1-59036-263-2 (pbk.)
 1. Biodegradation--Juvenile literature. I. Title. II. Series.
  QH530.5.L37 2004
  577'.16--dc22
                            2004012599

Printed in the United States of America
1 2 3 4 5 6 7 8 9 0   08 07 06 05 04

Project Coordinator Janice L. Redlin **Design and Layout** Bryan Pezzi
Copy Editor Heather C. Hudak **Photo Research** Simon Daykin

Photograph Credits
Every reasonable effort has been made to trace ownership and to obtain
permission to reprint copyright material. The publishers would be pleased
to have any errors or omissions brought to their attention so that they may
be corrected in subsequent printings.

Cover: mushroom (**Photos.com**); **CORBIS/MAGMA:** pages 6 (Clouds Hill Imaging), 10
(Howard Sochurek), 13T (Mike Buxton); **Corel Corporation:** pages 5R, 12, 15B, 20TR,
20BM; **Digital Vision Ltd.:** page 19T, 19B; **Photos.com:** pages 1, 3, 4, 5T, 5L, 5M, 5B,
7T, 7B, 8, 9T, 9B, 11T, 11B, 13B, 14T, 14B, 15T, 15M, 18, 20TL, 20TM, 20ML, 20MM, 20MR,
20BL, 20BR, 22.

On the Cover: Many mushrooms range in taste from bitter and earthy, to mild
and woody.

All of the Internet URLs given in the book were valid at the time of publication.
However, due to the dynamic nature of the Internet, some addresses may have
changed, or sites may have ceased to exist since publication. While the author
and publisher regret any inconvenience this may cause readers, no responsibility
for any such changes can be accepted by either the author or the publisher.

Contents

Nature's Food Chain

All living things need food to survive. Food provides the energy that plants and animals need to grow and thrive. Plants and animals do not rely on the same types of food to live. Plants make their own food. They use energy from the Sun and water from the soil. Some animals eat plants. Others eat animals that have already eaten plants. In this way, living things rely on each other and form a food chain.

A food chain is made up of **producers** and **consumers**. Plants are the only producers in the food chain. This is because they make energy. This energy can be used by the rest of the living things on Earth. The other living things are called consumers. There are four different types of consumers in a food chain. They are herbivores, carnivores, omnivores, and decomposers. All of the world's animals belong to one of these consumer groups. The fourth level of consumers in the food chain is called decomposers.

The first commercial mushroom farms were set up in caves in France in the mid-1600s.

Did you know?

If an animal's food source disappears, other animals will suffer and possibly die.

Food Chain Connections

The Sun

DECOMPOSER (consumer)

Omnivore (consumer)

Carnivore (consumer)

Herbivore (consumer)

Plant (producer)

What is a Decomposer?

Decomposers can be broken into two groups: decomposers and detritivores. Decomposers and detritivores are living things. They get their energy by eating and breaking down dead plants and animals. It takes many decomposers to break down decaying matter. Decomposers help keep an ecosystem clean by clearing away garbage created by dead matter. They are part of the **detritus food chain**. Decomposers are very small. They include tiny **bacteria** and **fungi**.

Bacteria adapt very well to the environment. They are found every place on Earth.

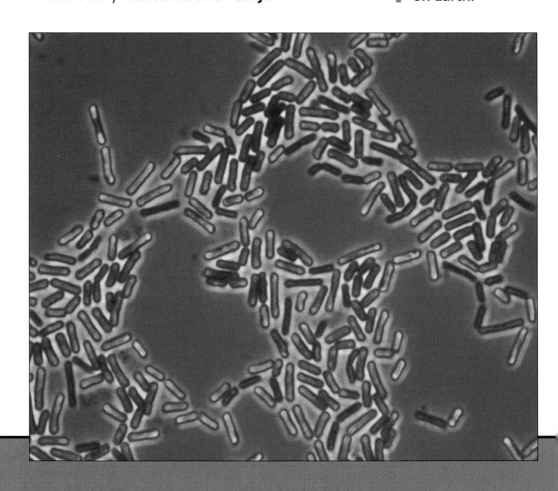

Animals that decompose dead plants and animals are called detritivores. They include earthworms, maggots, and termites.

Decomposers break down dead plants and animals using **enzymes**. The **nutrients** from this process pass into the air, soil, and water. Without decomposers, plants would not get the food they need to grow. As well, herbivores would not have plants to eat.

Some termites have special bacteria that live in their stomachs. The bacteria help break down food into sugars for energy.

Did you know?

Decomposers in a compost bin help turn leaves and leftover food into soil. Many decomposers, such as bacteria, are so small they cannot be seen by the human eye.

The Detritus Food Chain

Decomposers and detritivores are at the bottom of the food chain. They are very important because they eat **organic** material from dead plants and animals. They make this material into nutrients that help plants grow. This helps keep air and water clean.

Bacteria have recycled chemical compounds and elements on Earth for billions of years. Bacteria are among the earliest forms of life to live on Earth.

The process of breaking down matter begins with a detritivore, such as an earthworm. Earthworms break down dead material, or detritus, into smaller pieces. Then tiny decomposers, such as bacteria, complete the process. They make the detritus pieces even smaller. Soil and water absorb these small pieces. This **cycle** is repeated.

Bacteria produce the enzymes needed to build up and break down organic matter.

Parts of the detritus food chain:

detritus + detritivores + decomposers = nutrients for air, soil, and water

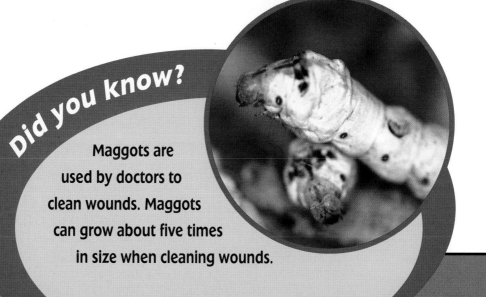

Did you know?

Maggots are used by doctors to clean wounds. Maggots can grow about five times in size when cleaning wounds.

Billions of Bacteria

Bacteria are everywhere. They are so tiny that millions of them could live in a space as small as the end of a pencil.

Scientists once believed bacteria were animals because they moved around. Scientists soon realized bacteria were not animals. They wondered if bacteria could be **classified** as plants instead. Now, scientists know that bacteria are neither plants nor animals. They are a class of their own.

About 100,000 individual bacteria can be found on 0.2 square inches (1 square centimeter) of human skin.

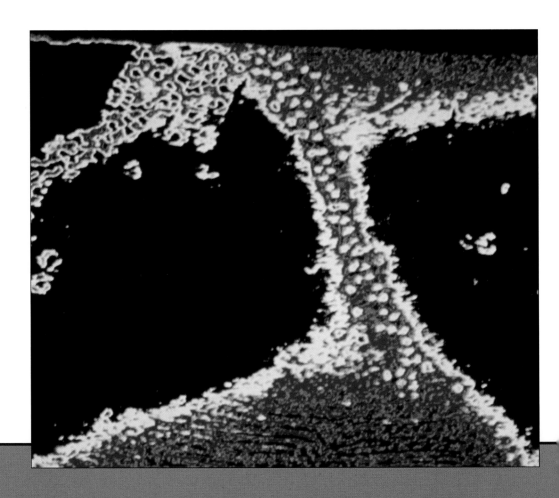

Bacteria that only eat dead plants and animals are decomposers. Bacteria make up the biggest group of decomposers. The work decomposers do is very important. Dead matter and waste would pile up if bacteria did not exist. Bacteria help plants get the important nutrients they need to survive.

When a plant dies, decomposers break down the dead organic material into energy and nutrients. The material is released into the air and soil for other living things to eat.

Did you know?

Some kinds of bacteria can live in very hot places. A type of bacteria called hyperthermofiles lives near volcano openings. Temperatures can rise to 212° Fahrenheit (100° Celsius) near these openings.

Freaky Fungi

Fungi are another type of decomposer. There are many different fungi. Some are very small. Some are huge—even as large as a dog. Most are not harmful, but a few are very dangerous. Two types of fungi are white destroying angel and deathcap mushrooms. They are part of the *amanita* family. This is the deadliest group of fungi on the planet. The umbrella-shaped form of a mushroom is the fruit of the fungus.

The only way to know which mushrooms are edible and which ones are poisonous is to learn to identify the different classes.

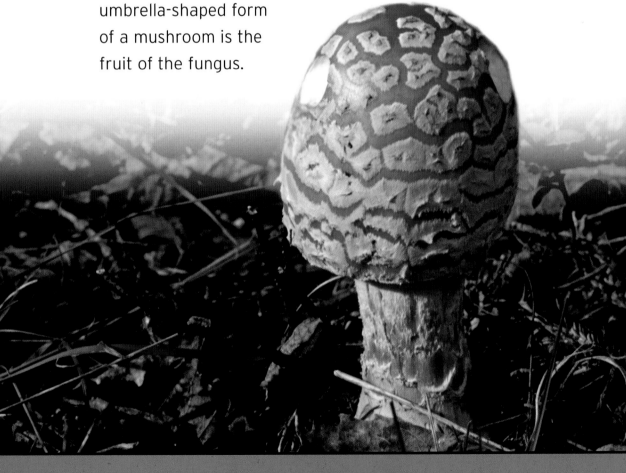

Some fungi are named after the foods they look like. For example, the "chicken of the woods" fungus looks similar to a big, yellow chicken. In Germany, people like to eat this fungus. Cooked chicken of the woods tastes much like chicken.

In early Roman times in Italy, upper-class people ate mushrooms at special events.

Did you know?

In the 1840s, fungi attacked potatoes in Ireland and caused a **famine**. Many people left the country because they did not have enough to eat. Some traveled overseas. Many people of Irish **descent** still live in the United States.

Decomposer Closeup

There are many different kinds of decomposers. Some, such as bacteria, are so tiny, they cannot be seen by the human eye. Detritivores, which include earthworms and millipedes, are large enough for human eyes to see without a **microscope**.

Decomposers can be found throughout the world. Some decomposers live in water. Many live on land.

Ascomycotines

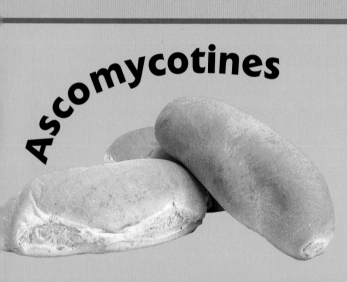

- the largest group of fungi
- found on dead animals, in fresh water, and in soil
- yeast is an ascomycotine used for making beer and baking
- ascomycotines are used to make the **antibiotic** penicillin, which is used to treat ear and throat infections

Maggots

- look like tiny, white worms
- **larvae** of the common housefly
- breathes using two small holes at their back end
- doctors use maggots to clean dead tissue from wounds

Mold

- tiny plants from the fungi family
- mold **spores** are always in the air
- molds are used to make some cheeses and vitamins
- mold grows best on soft fruits

Earthworms

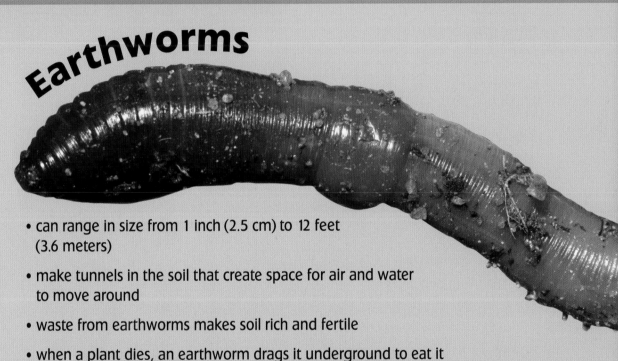

- can range in size from 1 inch (2.5 cm) to 12 feet (3.6 meters)
- make tunnels in the soil that create space for air and water to move around
- waste from earthworms makes soil rich and fertile
- when a plant dies, an earthworm drags it underground to eat it
- some people put worms in their compost bins, even indoors

Termites

- groups number from 100 to 1 million
- there are about 2,000 known **species**
- most build their nests underground
- sometimes known as white ants because of their color
- mainly eat wood

Decomposer Habitats

Decomposers live in many different places. They live in deserts, forests, and oceans. Some might even live in the refrigerator on a piece of moldy cheese or bread. The place where something lives is called its habitat.

Earth has many different habitats. A decomposer's habitat could be as large as a desert or an ocean. It could also be as small as a tree or a clump of soil.

Some of the world's largest habitats include deserts, grasslands, oceans, temperate forests, tropical rain forests, and tundra. Look at the map to see which types of decomposers live in each of these habitats. Can you think of other decomposers to add to each of these habitats?

Decomposers in the tundra: arctic tundra lichens, arctic tundra moss, bacteria

Decomposers in tropical rain forests: bacteria, fungi, millipedes, mold, termites

Decomposers in the ocean: bacteria, insect larvae, sea slugs, worms

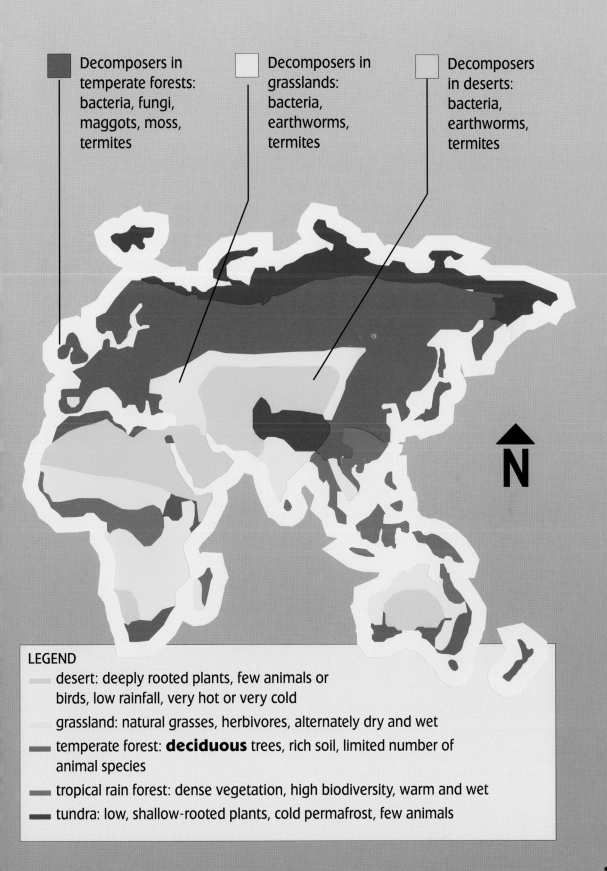

Decomposers in temperate forests: bacteria, fungi, maggots, moss, termites

Decomposers in grasslands: bacteria, earthworms, termites

Decomposers in deserts: bacteria, earthworms, termites

N

LEGEND

desert: deeply rooted plants, few animals or birds, low rainfall, very hot or very cold

grassland: natural grasses, herbivores, alternately dry and wet

temperate forest: **deciduous** trees, rich soil, limited number of animal species

tropical rain forest: dense vegetation, high biodiversity, warm and wet

tundra: low, shallow-rooted plants, cold permafrost, few animals

Nature's Recyclers

Without the work of decomposers, the world would be a messy place. Imagine if you had to wade through dead leaves, logs, and other dead things every day on your way to school. If not for decomposers, everything that died on Earth would keep piling up. Lakes and rivers would be clogged with dead fish.

There is more dead material, such as animals and plants, than living matter in bodies of water.

Decomposers have some very important jobs. They keep the world tidy. They also make sure nutrients from dead material are recycled back into the air, soil, and water. If there were no decomposers, the world would be very unpleasant. Nutrients would be trapped in the bodies of dead plants and animals. New plants would not be able to grow. Animals would have nothing to eat. Slowly, everything on Earth would die.

Water is necessary for decomposers to do their work. If an object does not contain water or is not exposed to water, it cannot decompose.

Did you know?

Decomposers, including bacteria, eat harmful chemicals that make their way into lakes and rivers. If there are too many chemicals in the water, decomposers cannot eat all of them. After some time, the water becomes very unhealthy.

Making a Food Chain

Animals, plants, and decomposers are linked together through a food chain. In this way, all living things depend on one another for survival. Each one of the decomposers below is part of its own unique food chain. Food chains that are connected are called food webs. Look closely at these decomposers. In what type of food chain do they belong? What does the decomposer eat? What animal eats it?

mushroom

yeast

deathcap

bacteria

mold

earthworm

maggot

termites

lichen

Once you have examined all of the pictured decomposers, pick one and learn more about it. Using the Internet and your school library, find information about the decomposer's diet. Is it a decomposer or a detritivore? Draw a food chain that shows what you learned. Write an explanation about how the decomposer fits into the food chain.

Do you have any decomposers in your house? Are there any decomposers in your garden? If so, write something about what the decomposer eats. Describe where you might find a decomposer.

One example of a food chain starts with a plant (producer). Large animals, such as giraffes (herbivores), live on plants. Giraffes are eaten by consumers. Energy is transferred from one living thing to another in a food chain.

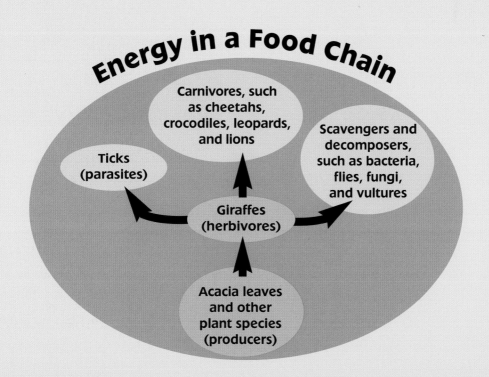

Energy in a Food Chain

Carnivores, such as cheetahs, crocodiles, leopards, and lions

Scavengers and decomposers, such as bacteria, flies, fungi, and vultures

Ticks (parasites)

Giraffes (herbivores)

Acacia leaves and other plant species (producers)

Quiz

Based on what you have just read, try to answer the following questions correctly.

1. What is a decomposer?

2. Give an example of a detritivore.

3. What is the umbrella-shaped form of a mushroom?

4. Are decomposers producers or consumers in the food chain?

5. What is detritus?

6. What group of fungi is the deadliest?

7. What do termites mainly eat?

8. Give one example of where bacteria might live.

Answers: 1. A living thing that gets its energy from eating dead plants and animals 2. Earthworm, maggot, or termite 3. The fruit of the fungus 4. Consumers 5. Dead material that decomposers eat 6. Fungi from the amanita family 7. Wood 8. In the ocean or in the soil

Further Research

There are many more interesting facts to learn about the world's decomposers. If you are interested in learning more, here are some places to start your research.

Web Sites

To learn more about nature and decomposers, visit:
www.nhptv.org/natureworks/nw4.htm

To find out about bacteria, visit:
www.nationalgeographic.com/ngkids/0010/bacteria

For more fascinating maggot facts, visit:
www.geocities.com/thesciencefiles/maggot/info.html

To learn more about worms and how to build your own recycling bin, visit:
http://yucky.kids.discovery.com/flash/worm

Books

McGinty, Alice B. and Dwight Kuhn. *Decomposers in the Food Chain*. New York: PowerKids Pr, 2002.

Silverstein, Alvin and Virginia Silverstein. *Life in a Bucket of Soil*. Mineola, NY: Dover Publications, 2000.

Glossary

antibiotic: substance used to hold back the growth of very small animals or plants, including bacteria and fungi

bacteria: one-celled animals or plants too small for the human eye to see

classified: similar things put together in one group

consumers: animals that feed on plants or other animals

cycle: something that is repeated

deciduous: type of tree with leaves that fall off each year

descent: a group of people whose relatives came from the same place

detritus food chain: living things, such as bacteria and earthworms, that work together to break down dead things

enzymes: protein that helps decomposition

famine: when there is not enough food to eat and people starve

fungi: plants that make small cells that reproduce, instead of seeds

larvae: wormlike babies of insects and some animals

microscope: an instrument with a lens for making small things look larger

nutrients: substances that provide food for plants and animals

organic: substances that come from plant or animal matter

producers: living things, such as plants, that produce their own food

species: a group of the same kind of living thing; members can breed together

spores: small cells that reproduce; used instead of seeds to make new fungi

Index